Mythical and Mysterious Creatures

Pamela Rushby

Mythical and Mysterious Creatures

Text: Nicolas Brasch
Publishers: Tania Mazzeo and Eliza Webb
Series consultant: Amanda Sutera

Hands on Heads Consulting
Editor: Sarah Layton
Project editor: Annabel Smith
Designer: Leigh Ashforth
Illustrations: Alessandra Fusi
Project designer: Danielle Maccarone
Permissions researchers: Lumina Datamatics
Production controller: Renee Tome

Acknowledgements
We would like to thank the following for permission to reproduce copyright material:

Front cover: Alessandra Fusi; p. 4: Todd Gipstein/The Image Bank Unreleased/Getty Images; p. 5 (top), (Index page): thanawong/Alamy Stock Photo, (bottom): Science History Images/Alamy Stock Photo; p. 7: CPA Media Pte Ltd/Alamy Stock Photo; p. 8 (top): CPA Media Pte Ltd/Alamy Stock Photo, (bottom): Pictures from History/Universal Images Group/Getty Images; p. 9 (top): Lebrecht Music & Arts/Alamy Stock Photo,(bottom): CBW/Alamy Stock Photo; p. 10: Alessandra Fusi; p. 11 (top): Penta Springs Limited/Alamy Stock Photo, (middle): Niday Picture Library/Alamy Stock Photo, (bottom): tom viggars/Alamy Stock Photo; p. 12, back cover: Alessandra Fusi; p. 13: Ivy Close Images/Alamy Stock Photo; p. 14: Alessandra Fusi; p. 15 (top): Renata Sedmakova/Shutterstock.com,(middle): J Marshall - Tribaleye Images/Alamy Stock Photo, (bottom): Album/Alamy Stock Photo; p. 17 (top): Areeya Yodplob/Alamy Stock Photo, (middle): Cavan Images/Alamy Stock Photo, (bottom): Edu Snacker/Shutterstock.com; pp. 18,19: (A & B IMAGES)/Private Collection/Bridgeman Images; p. 20 (top): Chronicle/Alamy Stock Photo, (bottom): Heritage Image Partnership Ltd/ Alamy Stock Photo; p. 21: Fox Photos/Hulton ArchiveGetty Images; p. 22, title page: Alessandra Fusi; p. 23 (top): AAP photos, (bottom): Adisha Pramod/Alamy Stock Photo; p. 25: David Chapman/Alamy Stock Photo; p. 27: SEAN GLADWELL/Moment/Getty Images; p. 28 (bottom): crbellette/Shutterstock.com; p. 29 (top): Album/Alamy Stock Photo, (bottom left): Science History Images/Alamy Stock Photo, (bottom right): sunemi Kubodera of the National Science Museum of Japan, HO/AAP Photos p. 30 (top): Zoonar GmbH/Alamy Stock Photo, (bottom): Jurgen Vogt/Shutterstock.com.

Every effort has been made to trace and acknowledge copyright. However, if any infringement has occurred, the publishers tender their apologies and invite the copyright holders to contact them.

NovaStar

ISBN 978 0 17 033497 6

Cengage Learning Australia
Level 5, 80 Dorcas Street
Southbank VIC 3006 Australia
Phone: 1300 790 853
Email: aust.nelsonprimary@cengage.com

For learning solutions, visit **cengage.com.au**

Printed in China by 1010 Printing International Ltd
1 2 3 4 5 6 7 29 28 27 26 25

Nelson acknowledges the Traditional Owners and Custodians of the lands of all First Nations Peoples. We pay respect to Elders past and present, and extend that respect to all First Nations Peoples today.

Contents

Myths and Mysteries

Since ancient times, people have wondered about the world around them. To explain things they did not understand, people created stories full of gods and heroes, and the **mythical** creatures they fought against – or that helped them. Stories like these are called **myths**. Fantastic stories of these animals spread across the ancient world, appearing in myths from many cultures. And the animals themselves – from the phoenix to unicorns and dragons – were said to have **supernatural** powers.

The Greek hero Heracles (pronounced *heh-ra-klees*), also known by the ancient Romans as Hercules, battled many mythical creatures including the hydra, a water monster.

It's not just in tales from long ago that stories about mysterious creatures can be found. Many people today still wonder about creatures that may, or may not, exist. Creatures like these are known as **cryptids**. People around the world report sightings of creatures like the **Loch** Ness Monster, Bigfoot and the Yowie. Some people even claim to have photographed or filmed these creatures. However, their existence has never been proven.

One rumoured cryptid called Mothman is a humanoid, mothlike creature with glowing eyes.

So, are these mysterious creatures just stories, like the mythical creatures of legend? Or could some cryptids actually exist? To find out, we need to delve into the world of mythical and mysterious creatures.

The bunyip is a cryptid from Aboriginal stories that lurks in billabongs.

CRYPTIDS – Stranger than Fiction?

Unlike the creatures from ancient myths, a cryptid is a mysterious creature that might not just be folklore. These beings, if they exist, are secretive and strange – and some people still believe in them.

Mythical Creatures

The Phoenix

The phoenix (pronounced *fee-nicks*) is one of the strangest and most well-known mythical creatures. Many cultures have myths that feature the phoenix. People in ancient Egypt, Greece, Rome, Japan, China, the Philippines, Persia (now Iran) and Arabia (now countries such as Jordan, Syria and Saudi Arabia) all told stories about an amazing fire bird.

While many cultures told stories of the phoenix, one thing all the different tales agreed on was that only one phoenix ever existed at a time. It lived all alone for between 500 and 1000 years. When the phoenix grew old and felt its end was near, it built a nest. It filled the nest with sweet-smelling spices. Then, it set itself on fire and burned to ashes. As the old bird disappeared, a new, young phoenix was reborn from the fire – and the cycle of life began again.

This artwork from the 19th century shows a phoenix in flames, ready to be reborn as a young bird.

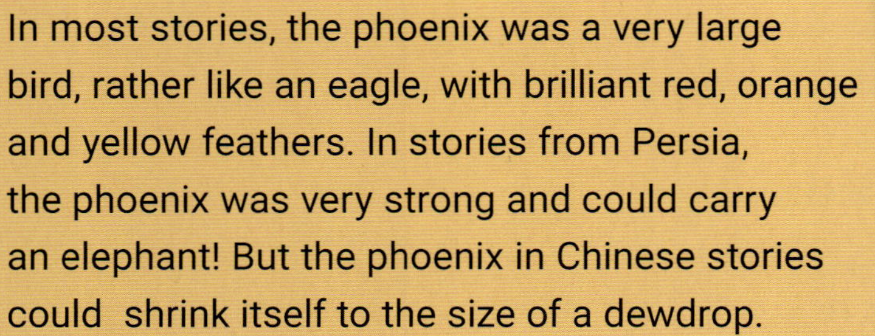

In most stories, the phoenix was a very large bird, rather like an eagle, with brilliant red, orange and yellow feathers. In stories from Persia, the phoenix was very strong and could carry an elephant! But the phoenix in Chinese stories could shrink itself to the size of a dewdrop.

The phoenix in Chinese stories had many heads, and it could shrink itself.

The phoenix in Persian stories could carry off elephants using its claws.

In stories from the Philippines, the phoenix had a sweet voice that could heal a sick person when it sang – but its droppings could turn living creatures to stone. The phoenix in Japanese stories brought good luck and gifts to those who heard its song. The phoenix in Greek stories also had a beautiful voice. Its song was so enchanting that the Greek Sun god, Helios (pronounced *hee-lee-os*), would pause his chariot's journey across the sky just to listen.

Helios drove his chariot from East to West, causing the Sun to rise and set.

The Phoenix Today

The phoenix is still represented in pop culture today. The *Harry Potter* series of books and films features a phoenix named Fawkes. There is also a phoenix in the 2020 film *Mulan.*

Unicorns

Unicorns have captured people's imaginations for thousands of years. They are mythical animals that look like pure white horses with a horn growing out of the middle of their foreheads. Unicorns appear in myths from ancient **Mesopotamia** (modern-day Iraq), India, Greece and Europe.

In **medieval** Europe, unicorns were believed to be fierce and dangerous. They fought with their hooves and their horn. The horn of a unicorn, crushed to powder and used as a medicine, was thought to be magical. It could heal sickness and get rid of poison.

In ancient Greek and medieval stories about unicorns, hunters often tried to catch them for their horns. However, the hunters found that, no matter what they did, they could not catch a unicorn – it could only be caught by a young girl. When a **maiden** approached a unicorn, it would surrender to her and lay its head in her lap. Then, the maiden could put a rope around the unicorn's neck and lead it away.

Unicorns also had the power to purify water with their horn.

Unicorns could only be caught and tamed by a young woman.

Unicorns Today

Unicorns are popular today in books and films, as toys, or printed on clothing. But these unicorns are not **depicted** as dangerous. They're often shown as cute and cuddly, rainbow-coloured, and with big eyes.

Sphinxes

Sphinxes are mythical creatures with the body of a lion and the head of a human. Many cultures have myths that include sphinxes. It is thought that sphinxes like to tell **riddles**.

The ancient Egyptians had many stories about sphinxes. They made statues of them that were placed as guardians to protect pyramids, temples and tombs. One path in Egypt between the great temples of Luxor and Karnak is called "Sphinx Alley", because it is lined with sphinx statues.

The most famous statue of a sphinx in the world is over 4500 years old, and you can still see it in Egypt today. It's the Great Sphinx at Giza in Cairo. The statue is 73 metres long – about as long as six buses. Its huge paws are nearly as tall as two people. Archaeologists think it was built during the time of the **pharaoh** Khafre (pronounced *kaf-ray*), and that it has his face.

The ancient Greeks also told stories of sphinxes. Greek sphinxes were female, and they were believed to be treacherous and **merciless**. Depictions of sphinxes were often placed on graves to frighten away grave robbers. These sphinxes had the head of a woman, the body of a lion and the wings of a bird – and they could fly.

The Riddle of the Sphinx

A sphinx played an important role in the ancient Greek story about how Oedipus (pronounced *ee-duh-puhs*), the king of Thebes, **ascended** to the throne. The city of Thebes was being tormented by a sphinx. The sphinx challenged the young men of Thebes to answer a riddle: *What walks on four legs in the morning, two legs at noon and three legs in the evening?* Many tried to answer the riddle and failed. Then, the sphinx would eat them.

The people of Thebes were so desperate to get rid of the sphinx, they promised the throne of Thebes to any man who could solve the riddle. Oedipus guessed the answer. In a rage, the sphinx threw herself off the city walls, and Oedipus became king of Thebes.

Can you guess the answer to the riddle? The answer is *a human*. (Humans crawl on all fours as babies, walk upright as an adult and lean on a stick in old age.)

Oedipus solved the riddle of the sphinx.

Dragons

Dragons are evil, lizard-like mythical creatures that collect treasure and fly over human towns breathing fire. Well, not always. There are stories of dragons from all parts of the world, and the dragons can be very different.

In many tales, dragons are huge creatures with scaly skin, sharp teeth, clawed feet and wings that look like the wings of a bat. They can breathe fire or poison. They attack villages and humans and steal cattle. In European stories, a hero often bravely fights and **slays** the dragon.

However, in stories from China and Japan, dragons are friendly and bring good luck. They have no wings, but they can still fly. Dragons are water creatures, and they control wind, rain and rivers.

A dragon was the symbol of the emperors of ancient China. The emperors were believed to be descended from dragons. Today, dancers in dragon costumes bring good luck at Chinese festivals, like the Lunar New Year.

Knights fought evil dragons to protect people.

Dragons were used as a symbol by the emperors of China.

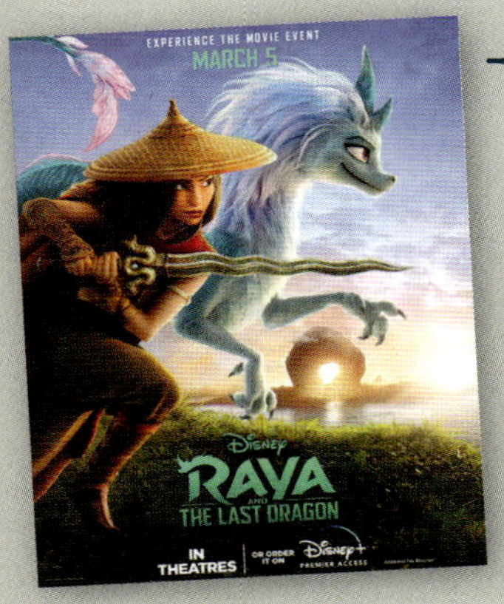

Dragons Today

You'll find many dragons in stories and films. European-style dragons appear in C.S. Lewis's Narnia books and J.R.R. Tolkien's *The Hobbit*. More recently, the film *Raya and the Last Dragon* shows a dragon based on Southeast Asian myths (China and Japan). A reptile called the Komodo Dragon, from the island of Komodo in Indonesia, takes its name from the dragon because it's thought to resemble one!

Kitsune

The name kitsune (pronounced *kit-soo-neh*) comes from the Japanese word for "fox". In Japanese mythology, kitsune are mythical trickster spirits in the form of foxes. Kitsune can also shape-shift into a human form, and some can control fire.

According to Japanese stories, kitsune can live for hundreds of years. As they get older, they grow more tails. Some can have up to nine tails. There are two types of kitsune: zenko (good) and nogitsune (bad).

Good fox spirits, zenko, serve as messengers for the rice god, Inari. Inari is the protector of rice cultivation and is sometimes pictured riding a white fox. **Shrines** to Inari have many fox statues. They wear little red bibs to chase away demons and illness. These kitsune are playful and will not harm humans.

A statue of a good fox spirit guards a shrine to Inari in Japan.

Nogitsune are not so friendly. They can be mischievous, and they play tricks on humans. There are mythical Japanese stories about a nogitsune that turns itself into a beautiful woman and marries a human. But the stories usually have a sad ending, as the nogitsune eventually turns back into a fox before running away.

Nogitsune can appear in the form of a beautiful woman.

Kitsune Today

Kitsune are very popular in Japanese stories today. They appear in **anime** and video games. The fox character Miles "Tails" Prower in Sonic the Hedgehog is a kitsune. Miles has only two tails, which means he is quite young. The Pokemon "Ninetales" is also a kitsune.

Ninetales, from Pokemon

Mysterious Creatures: CRYPTIDS

THE LOCH NESS MONSTER

For nearly 1500 years, there has been a story that a huge monster lives in the depths of Loch Ness, a large, very deep lake in Scotland. It's said to have a long neck, a small head and a humped back that rises out of the water. But is it just a myth?

The first person to write about seeing the monster was Saint Columba, in 565 CE. The saint wrote that he was travelling in Scotland, on the banks of Loch Ness, when he saw a huge beast in the water about to attack a man who was swimming. Saint Columba commanded the monster to "Go back with all speed!" The monster obeyed, and the man was saved.

Saint Columba is said to have first seen the Loch Ness Monster.

Since then, there have been many reported sightings of the monster. In 1933, a man and his wife said they saw it crossing a road by the loch. In 1934, a doctor said he had photographed a monster in the water. The picture was published in the *Daily Mail* newspaper. Many years later, this photograph was discovered to be a fake. Still, over the years, hundreds of people have looked for the monster.

This photo of the Loch Ness Monster taken by Dr Robert Wilson was later proven to be fake.

"WE SAW THE MONSTER!"

"Daily Mail" Mission

Adventure of Our Loch Ness Party

WHAT WAS THE BIG DARK OBJECT?

NET

A 12

The Daily achievement— approached by

It is the st —beginning w popularity of a

Reports of Loch Ness Monster sightings have made front-page news.

Universities and television networks have sent expeditions to the loch, searching for the monster with **sonar** equipment. The latest search was in 2023, using drones, cameras and underwater **hydrophones**. The expedition discovered large moving objects deep in the loch, but the evidence was not conclusive.

There are many theories about what the monster could be: groups of seals, dolphins, a giant lamprey eel or even a water-dwelling dinosaur that has survived to the current day. But no one knows for sure.

Members of the Loch Ness Monster Investigation Team searched Loch Ness in 1968.

BIGFOOT, YETIS AND YOWIES

Countries all over the world have stories of huge, hairy, ape-like creatures that can be up to 4.5 metres tall. They live in remote, wild areas and avoid contact with humans.

In the Himalayan mountains in Asia, there are stories of a creature called the Abominable Snowman, or the Yeti. In Canada and the USA, it's known as Bigfoot, or the Sasquatch. In Australia, creatures like this are called Yowie.

The Abominable Snowman is said to have shaggy white fur that lets it blend into its snowy environment. Some people even wonder whether it could be a living descendant of prehistoric humans, like Neanderthals. But scientists think this is unlikely.

This image is from the video taken by Robert Patterson in 1967, and shows a large, hairy figure.

The first claimed sighting of Bigfoot was in 1811 by an explorer in Canada. He saw enormous footprints that he believed were made by a wild man. In 1967, a man named Roger Patterson claimed to have filmed Bigfoot near Bluff Creek in California, USA. In 2012, a hiker in Utah, USA, reported that a strange, two-legged, hairy creature had thrown rocks at him.

In Australia, there are many reports of the Yowie, a wild creature that lives in the outback and coastal bush. Yowies are said to be tall and covered in thick hair, with very long arms. Some reports say their feet are turned backwards, so they are very hard to track.

An artist's interpretation of a Yowie shows its long arms and fur-covered body.

A man named Tony Duffy claims he has taught some English to a large male Yowie living in the bush near the town of Gympie in Queensland. A newspaper, *The Gympie Times*, reported that Mr Duffy said he had encountered Yowies seven times, and that they were peaceful and needed protection.

BIG CATS

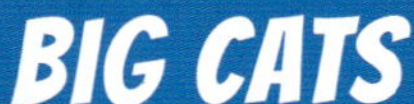

Ever since 1760, there have been stories of large, mysterious, cat-like creatures roaming the English countryside. They have been given names like the Fen Tiger, the Beast of Bodmin and the Surrey Puma.

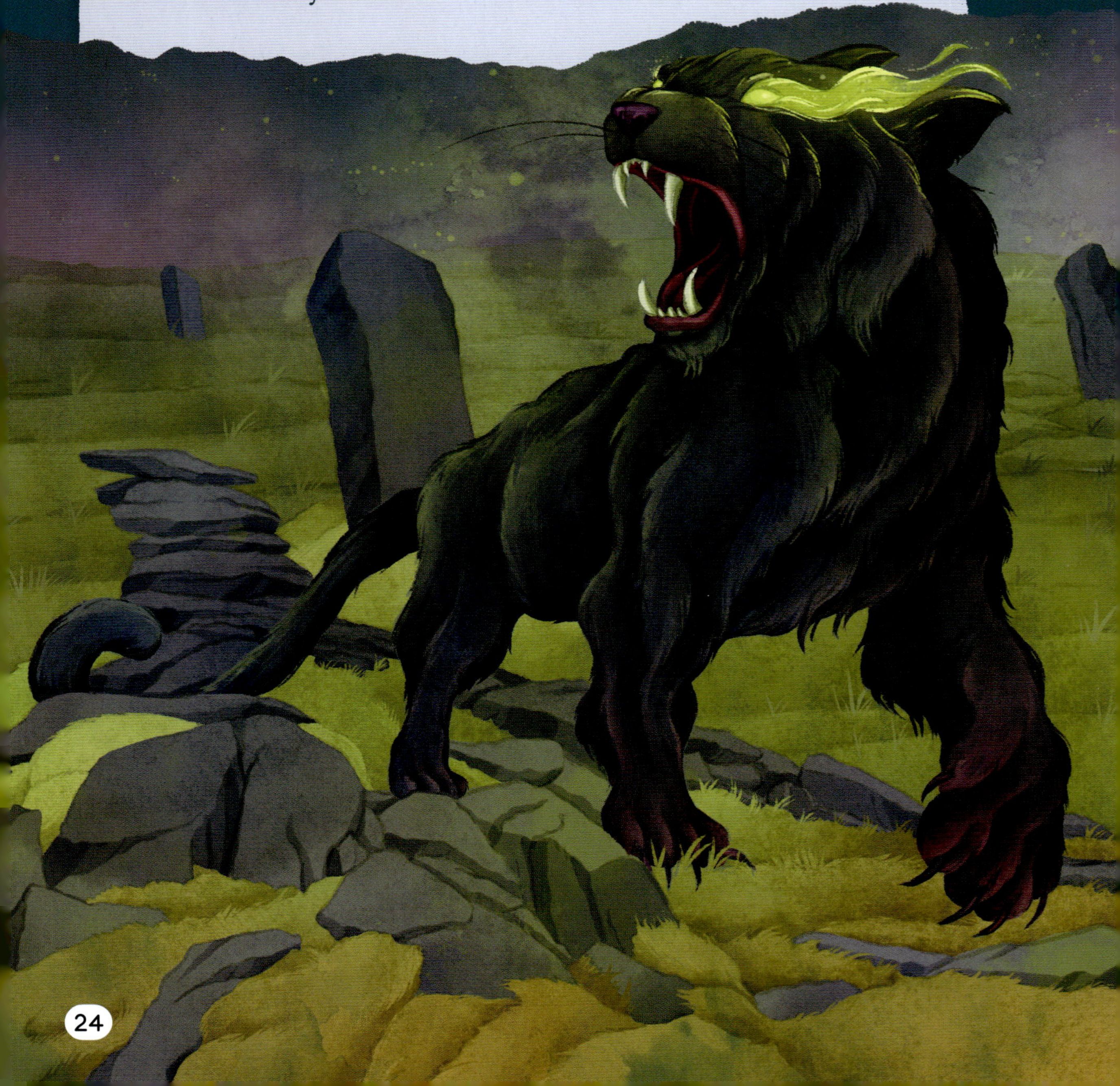

The first recorded sighting of a mysterious big cat was by the writer William Corbett, who said he had seen a giant black cat in Surrey, England. This cat came to be known as the Surrey Puma, but it was never found.

A huge, black, panther-like cat was also reported to be roaming Bodmin Moor in Cornwall, England, in 1978. Farmers had found dead livestock that they said looked as if the animals had been attacked by a lion or tiger. Over the years, there were more than 60 reports of a cat-like creature by people who had seen it at a distance, or who said they had been chased by it. In 1995, the government ordered an investigation. No real evidence of a big cat was found on Bodmin Moor. But, the report stated, there was no real evidence *against* such a creature existing either.

Grazing farm animals on Bodmin Moor would make a good meal for a big cat.

Another big cat may have existed in Cambridgeshire, England – the Fen Tiger. It was first reported in 1978. The *Cambridge News* website listed many sightings of the Fen Tiger in the 1980s and 1990s, and again, farm animals were killed.

Even though it sounds unlikely, big cats may actually be roaming around the English countryside. DNA from black hairs caught on a barbed wire fence near a sheep attack were sent for testing in 2023. The laboratory that tested the hair reported it was a 99 per cent match to a big cat species.

Still to Be Solved

Over time, people have travelled more widely and learnt more about the world. Creatures that appeared in the myths of many cultures, such as unicorns, dragons and sphinxes, are no longer believed to be real. But others – well, people aren't so sure. Some creatures are perhaps not quite as imaginary as people think. Perhaps cryptids like the Loch Ness Monster, Bigfoot and big cats may turn out to be real after all.

Dragon

Phoenix

Unicorn

Sphinx

Yeti

Kitsune

People still report sightings of mysterious creatures, and searches for them go on. Many people still watch out for cryptids and try to prove they exist.

Even today, there are still mysteries to be solved.

Some animals were once believed to be mythical or made up, but later turned out to be ***ABSOLUTELY REAL!***

THE IMPOSSIBLE ANIMAL

In 1797, an animal that was said to be "impossible" was found to be quite real. Captain John Hunter, governor of the colony of New South Wales, Australia, saw an Aboriginal hunter spear a strange animal. He sent its skin and a drawing of the animal back to Britain.

This painting by John Gould in 1863 shows how strange platypuses must have looked to British colonists.

Naturalists there could not believe that such an incredible animal could exist. They thought Hunter's report was a joke, and that the creature was something from an Aboriginal myth. An animal with a beak like a duck, a fur-covered body with webbed feet and that laid eggs – impossible! But the animal was quite real. We know it today as a platypus.

A platypus swims through the water using its tail and webbed feet.

Monsters from THE DEEP

This Greek pottery depicts the sea monster Scylla.

Many cultures have centuries-old stories of enormous sea monsters. The ancient Greeks told stories about a giant, six-headed sea creature named Scylla (pronounced *sil-ah*). She protected her cave fiercely and harmed anyone who came near it. A story from the Bahamas, near Central America, said that a half-shark, half-octopus monster called Lusca lived in the seas around the islands. Other stories from Scandinavia spoke of the kraken, an enormous creature with long tentacles that attacked ships and ate their crews.

These monsters were all believed to be mythical. Then, in 1853, a Norwegian naturalist found a giant squid with long tentacles washed up on a beach in Norway. Creatures like this could be where the stories of sea monsters began.

The mythological Norse kraken attacked ships.

A giant squid attacks a bait.

HUGELY POWERFUL CREATURES

For many years, early travellers in Africa told tales of dark, hairy, human-like creatures that had come close to their camps. The creatures were said to have the strength of ten humans, but no one knew what they were. Then, in 1847, the Reverend Thomas Savage, a missionary in Africa, brought some unusual skulls home with him to New York City in the USA. The skulls resembled those of monkeys, but they were much, much larger. They were a totally new species that scientists named gorillas.

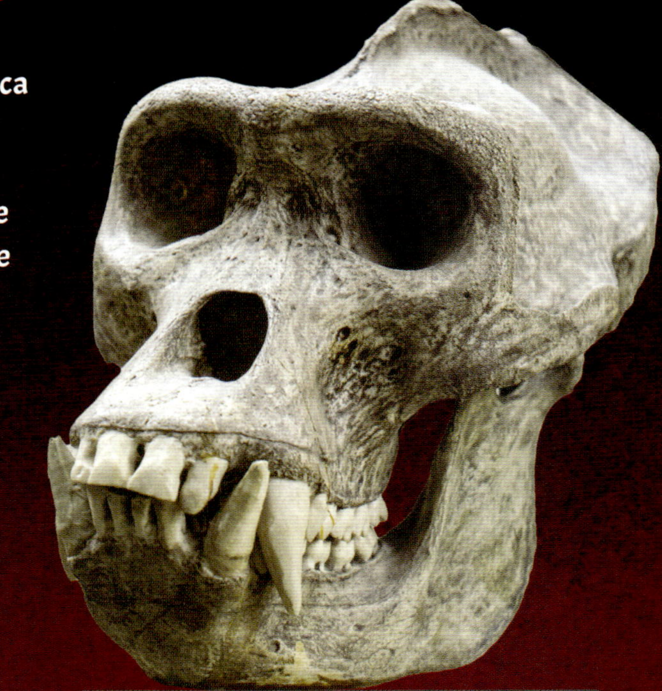

This gorilla skull is similar to the ones discovered by Rev Thomas Savage.

Gorillas and humans are closely related and extremely similar.

Glossary

anime (*noun*)	animated, cartoon-like film and television from Japan
ascended (*verb*)	rose to a higher rank or position
cryptids (*noun*)	a group of creatures whose existence is disputed
depicted (*verb*)	shown through a picture or artwork
folklore (*noun*)	the stories of a country or community
hydrophones (*noun*)	underwater microphones
loch (*noun*)	the Scottish word for a lake or narrow area of sea surrounded by land
maiden (*noun*)	a girl or young woman who is not married
medieval (*adjective*)	from the Middle Ages (from around the 5th to the 15th centuries)
merciless (*adjective*)	without sympathy or kindness
Mesopotamia (*noun*)	ancient Iraq
missionary (*noun*)	a person sent to a foreign place to teach people about a religion, often Christianity
mythical (*adjective*)	from myths, not real
myths (*noun*)	ancient stories that are not true
naturalists (*noun*)	people who study nature and the environment
pharaoh (*noun*)	a king of ancient Egypt
riddles (*noun*)	tricky questions that can be asked as a game that have a surprising answer
shrines (*noun*)	places to pray or make religious offerings
slays (*verb*)	kills or defeats
sonar (*noun*)	equipment used to locate underwater objects using sound
supernatural (*adjective*)	magical or unable to be explained
tentacles (*noun*)	long, thin arms on some creatures

Index

Going Deep About Sleep

Cameron Macintosh

Going Deep About Sleep

Text: Cameron Macintosh
Publishers: Tania Mazzeo and Eliza Webb
Series consultant: Amanda Sutera
Hands on Heads Consulting
Editor: Sarah Layton
Project editor: Annabel Smith
Designer: Leigh Ashforth
Project designer: Danielle Maccarone
Permissions researchers: Lumina Datamatics
Production controller: Renee Tome

Acknowledgements
We would like to thank the following for permission to reproduce copyright material:

Front cover: Carlos Caetano/Adobe Stock Photos; p. 4: LWA/Dann Tardif/Getty Images; p. 5: (top) PeopleImages.com - Yuri A/Shutterstock.com; (bottom) Kateryna Kon/Shutterstock.com; p. 6: BearFotos/Shutterstock.com; p. 7: iStock.com/eyecrave productions; p. 8: (top) FamVeld/Shutterstock.com (bottom) Zurijeta/Shutterstock.com; p. 9: (top left) Design Pics Inc/Alamy Stock Photo; (top right) Tetra Images/Getty Images; (bottom) miniseries/E+/Getty Images; p. 10: (top) (Index page) Ena Taly/Shutterstock.com; (bottom) ADDICTIVE STOCK CREATIVES/Alamy Stock Photo; p. 11: Realstock/Shutterstock.com; p. 12: Lysenko Andrii/Shutterstock.com; p. 13: Motortion Films/Shutterstock.com; p. 14: Drobot Dean/Adobe Stock Photos; p. 15: Prostock-studio/Alamy Stock Photo; p. 16: Science Photo Library/Alamy Stock Photo; p. 17: iStock.com/magicmine; p. 18: Andrey_Popov/Shutterstock.com; p. 19: John B Hewitt/Shutterstock.com; p. 20: iStock.com/FG Trade; p. 21: (top) Baravonda/Shutterstock.com, (bottom) Pixel-shot/Alamy Stock Photo; p. 22: (top) Gorodenkoff/Shutterstock.com; (bottom) FG Trade/E+/Getty Images; p. 23: JPC-PROD/Adobe Stock Photos; p. 24: Juliya Shangarey/Shutterstock.com; p. 25: (top) vetre/Adobe Stock Photos; (bottom) The History Collection/Alamy Stock Photo; p. 26: (top) bsd studio/Shutterstock.com; (bottom) Riska/E+/Getty Images; p. 27: (top) Pekic/E+/Getty Images; (bottom) evrim ertik/E+/Getty Images; p. 28: (top) Markus Wegmann/Alamy Stock Photo; (bottom) Tetra Images, LLC/Alamy Stock Photo; p. 29 (top) (title page) Elena Abrosimova/Alamy Stock Photo; (bottom) ohrim/Adobe Stock Photos; p. 30: Esther Moreno/Alamy Stock Photo.

Every effort has been made to trace and acknowledge copyright. However, if any infringement has occurred, the publishers tender their apologies and invite the copyright holders to contact them.

NovaStar

ISBN 978 0 17 033496 9

Cengage Learning Australia
Level 5, 80 Dorcas Street
Southbank VIC 3006 Australia
Phone: 1300 790 853
Email: aust.nelsonprimary@cengage.com

For learning solutions, visit **cengage.com.au**

Printed in China by 1010 Printing International Ltd
1 2 3 4 5 6 7 29 28 27 26 25

Nelson acknowledges the Traditional Owners and Custodians of the lands of all First Nations Peoples. We pay respect to Elders past and present, and extend that respect to all First Nations Peoples today.

Contents

What Is Sleep?

We all know how it feels to get sleepy and to fall asleep. We also know how much better we can feel after a good night's sleep, or even a short nap. But what actually is sleep, and what does it do for us?

Although a lot is still unknown about sleep, scientists have learnt that sleep is a time of deep rest, in which our bodies and brains recover from the work they have done during the day. It's also a time for our brains and bodies to prepare for the day to come. Sleep is particularly important for children, because it's during sleep that our bodies grow.

Children need to sleep more and longer than adults to help their bodies grow.

Scientists are discovering more about sleep all the time. They have learnt that many complex **processes** happen in our brains and bodies while we sleep. For example, new information learnt during the day is stored in our brains so that we can remember it in the future. Memories of things we have experienced during the day are stored away, too. Scientists have also learnt that sleep is **essential** to the health of our brains and bodies.

Getting the right amount of sleep gives us the energy we need to have fun during the day.

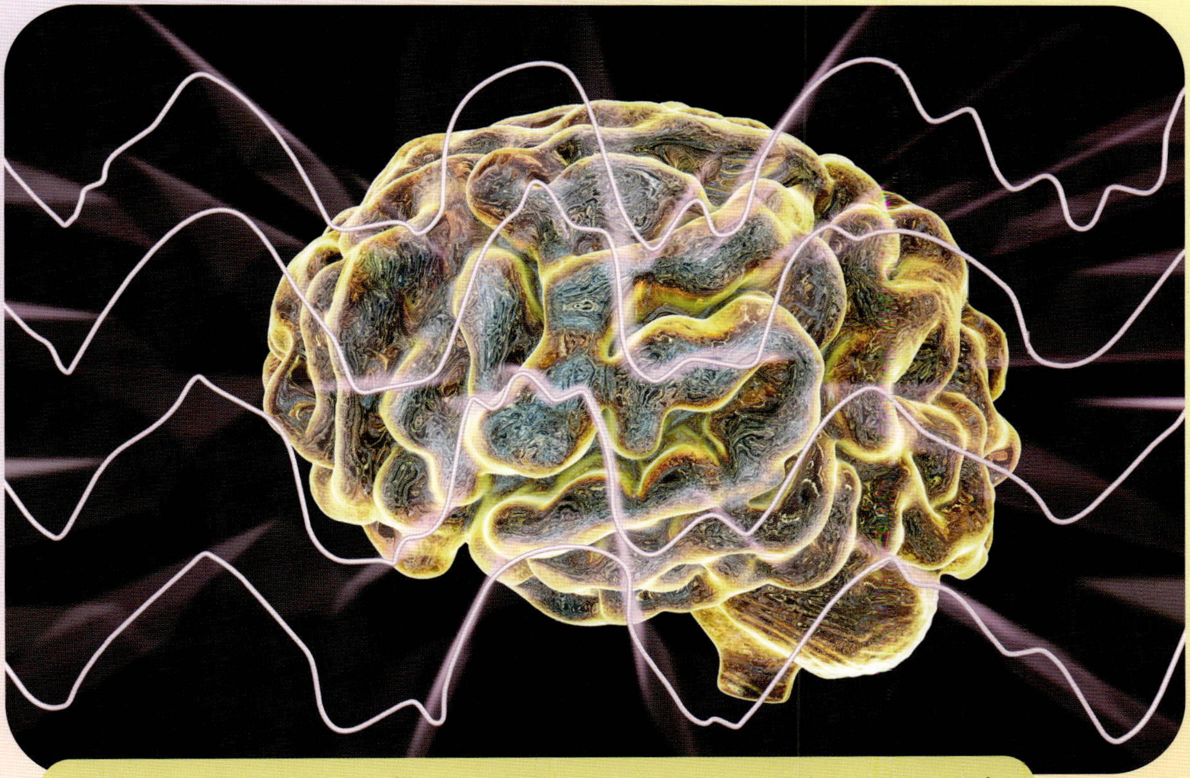

Scientists use a test called an EEG to map brain activity on a graph.

If we don't get enough sleep, our brains can't work to the best of their abilities. For example, we might struggle to think clearly. We might also feel sudden changes in our **mood**, and even changes in our **perception** – the way we experience the world through our senses of touch, taste, smell, sight and hearing. After several days without sleep, people can even experience hallucinations, where they see, hear or smell things that aren't there.

If you don't get enough sleep at night, you can quickly start to feel tired during the day and struggle to concentrate.

Poor **quality** sleep can negatively affect the way our bodies work, too. For example, not getting enough sleep or having an interrupted sleep can affect our **immune system**. Our immune system protects our body from harmful **viruses**, **bacteria** and other toxic substances. If we don't get enough sleep, our immune system can weaken, and these harmful invaders can have a higher chance of making us sick.

If we don't get enough sleep, our immune systems can be affected, leading to a higher chance of getting sick.

Sleep Throughout Our Lives

To get all of the benefits of sleep and to avoid the problems that come with lack of sleep, we need different amounts of it at different times in our lives.

From Birth to One Year Old

In the first year of our lives, we need about 10 to 18 hours of sleep each day. For the first two months of their lives, babies sleep almost as much during the day as they do during the night.

One to Five Years Old

Toddlers (children between the ages of one and three) and other young children usually sleep for 10 to 14 hours each day, including naps. Toddlers tend to have a nap in the morning and a nap in the afternoon. By the age of five, most children no longer need a daytime nap.

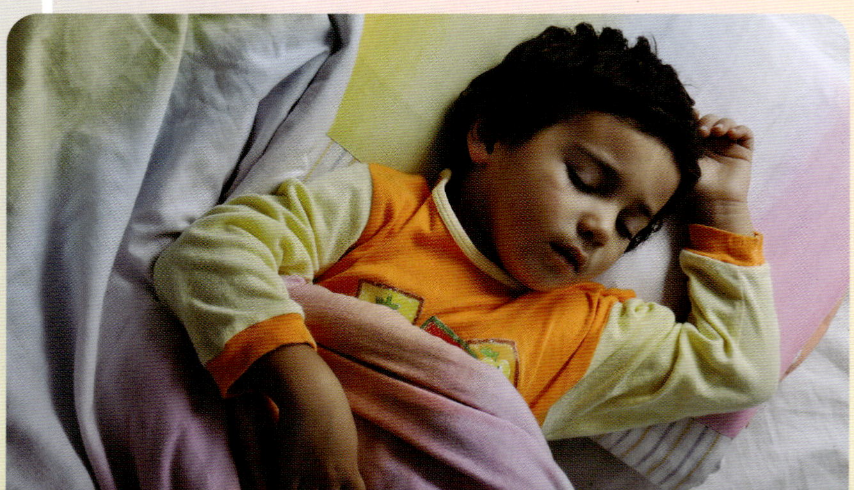

Six to Twelve Years Old

Most children between the ages of six and 12 need between 9 and 11 hours of sleep each night. By this age, they are sleeping in a similar way to most adults – having a solid sleep at night-time without the need for daytime naps.

Thirteen to Eighteen Years Old

Most teenagers between the ages of 13 and 18 need between 9 and 11 hours of sleep. They tend to get tired later at night, so they go to sleep later and wake later in the morning than younger children and adults.

Adults

Most adults need between 7 and 9 hours of sleep each night.

SLEEP FACT

We spend about a third of our lives asleep. In other words, a person who lives to the age of 75 will spend about 25 of those years asleep!

The Stages of Sleep

Scientists have observed four distinct stages in a regular night's sleep. These stages last for different amounts of time. The length of the stages can vary a lot between different people, too. Scientists are still studying these stages, and trying to find out the purpose each of them serves.

1. Lightest sleep
2. Light sleep
3. Deep sleep
4. REM (Rapid Eye Movement) sleep

Stage 1 – Lightest Sleep

The first stage of sleep is a time of light sleep. In this stage, we move from being wide awake to falling asleep. This stage is usually the shortest, only lasting a few minutes – seven at most. During this stage, our heart rate, brain activity and eye movements all begin to slow down. We can still be easily awoken.

Stage 2 – Light Sleep

During the second stage of sleep, we begin to sleep more deeply. Our heart rate, brain activity and eye movements continue to slow down, as does our breathing. Our body temperature might also drop. This stage can last between 10 and 25 minutes, but it is also the stage of sleep we experience the most throughout the night – about half of all our time asleep.

10–25
minutes

SLEEP FACT

Have you ever fallen asleep and then woken up again with a feeling like you're falling? Don't worry! That's just your body making sure you're in a good position before moving into Stage 3 sleep.

Stage 3 – Deep Sleep

In the third stage of sleep, our breathing, heart rate and brain activity are at their most relaxed. Our muscles are at their most relaxed, too. We are now sleeping deeply. During this stage of sleep, our bodies do most of their rest, repair and growth. One way our bodies do this is by releasing growth **hormones**. Our immune systems are also boosted during this stage. This stage usually lasts between 20 and 40 minutes.

Stage 4 – REM Sleep

The fourth stage of sleep is also known as rapid eye movement (REM) sleep. This is because during this stage, our eyes move rapidly backwards and forwards under our eyelids. We do most of our dreaming during this stage of sleep, and our dreams are at their most **vivid**. Both our heart rate and our breathing speed up again during this stage, but will still likely be more relaxed than when we are awake. This stage usually lasts between 10 and 60 minutes.

Scientists believe that REM sleep is particularly important in helping us process our emotions and store memories. We spend less time in this stage of sleep each night as we get older.

SLEEP FACT

During REM sleep, we are **temporarily** unable to move our arms and legs. Scientists think this prevents us from physically acting out our dreams and hurting ourselves or others while we sleep.

Our Brains During Sleep

Although sleep is a time of relaxation, it's also a very busy time for our brains. As we cycle through the stages of sleep, our brains perform all sorts of important functions.

One important function is that during sleep, memories of things that we learnt and experienced during the day are organised and stored away in our brains in ways that help us continue to remember them.

Clearly remembering the things we learnt yesterday and the day before is important to building skills and knowledge.

Sleep, particularly during the REM stage, also gives our brains the chance to process our emotional memories from the day so that we aren't **overwhelmed**. As we dream in REM sleep, our brains work through the emotions we've been feeling. While dreaming, our brains store positive emotions, such as excitement and happiness, and help us to let go of negative emotions, such as fear, anger or disappointment.

Each day, people feel a huge range of emotions.

Brain Washing!

Another important thing that happens during sleep is that our brains wash themselves in fluids that clear away harmful waste. This waste comes from the **cells** in our brains. To survive, the cells **consume** substances including sugar and oxygen. This makes the cells produce waste, similar to how animals produce waste after eating and digesting food. The waste builds up in our brains and needs to be removed.

Our brains work extremely hard and need lots of energy.

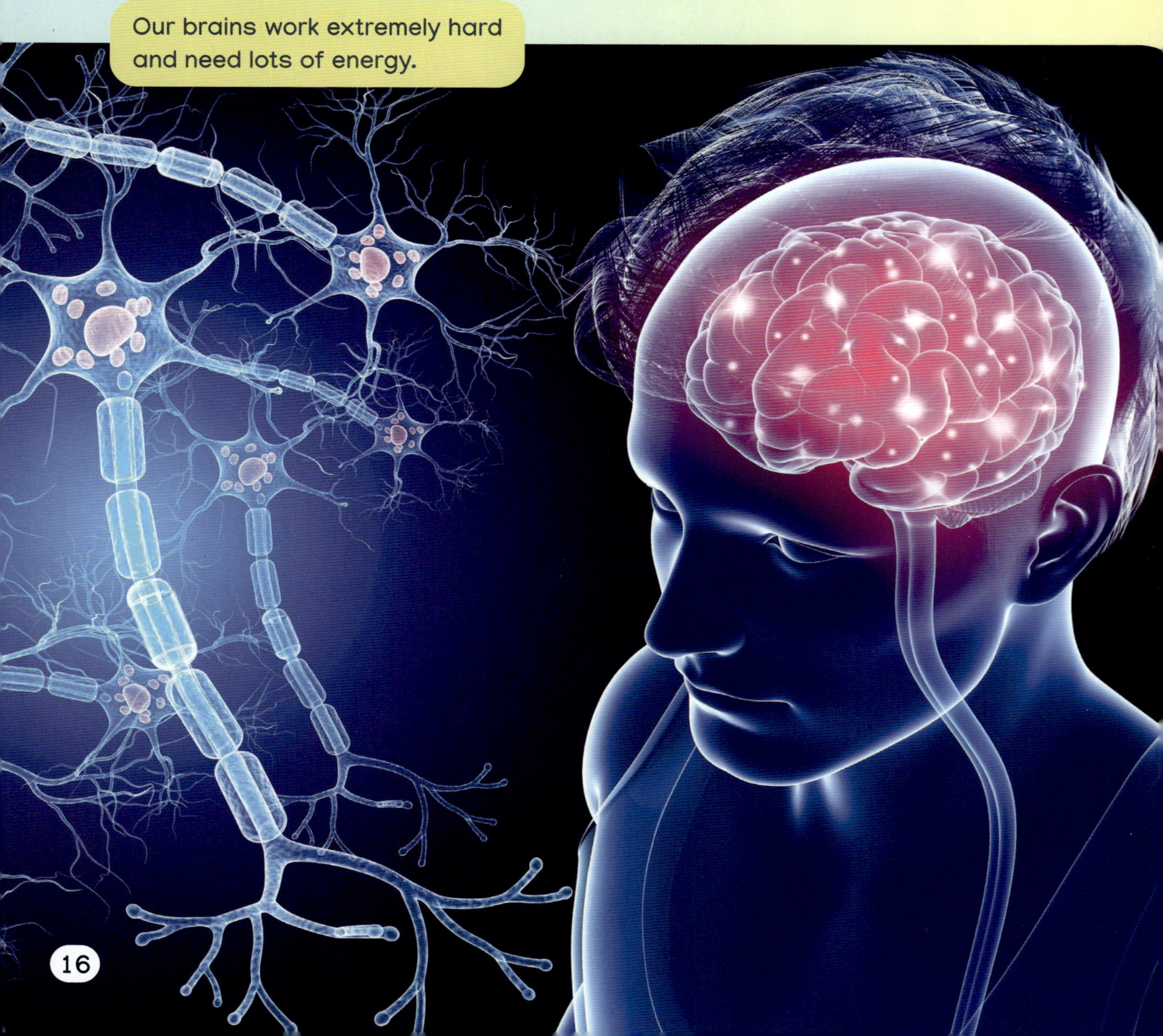

A system of tubes known as the **glymphatic system** flushes fluids past our brain cells and washes away this waste. This helps to keep our brains healthy, and it might help prevent brain illnesses, like **Alzheimer's disease** and **Parkinson's disease**. This washing happens mostly while we are in deep sleep, in the third stage of sleep.

How the Glymphatic System Works

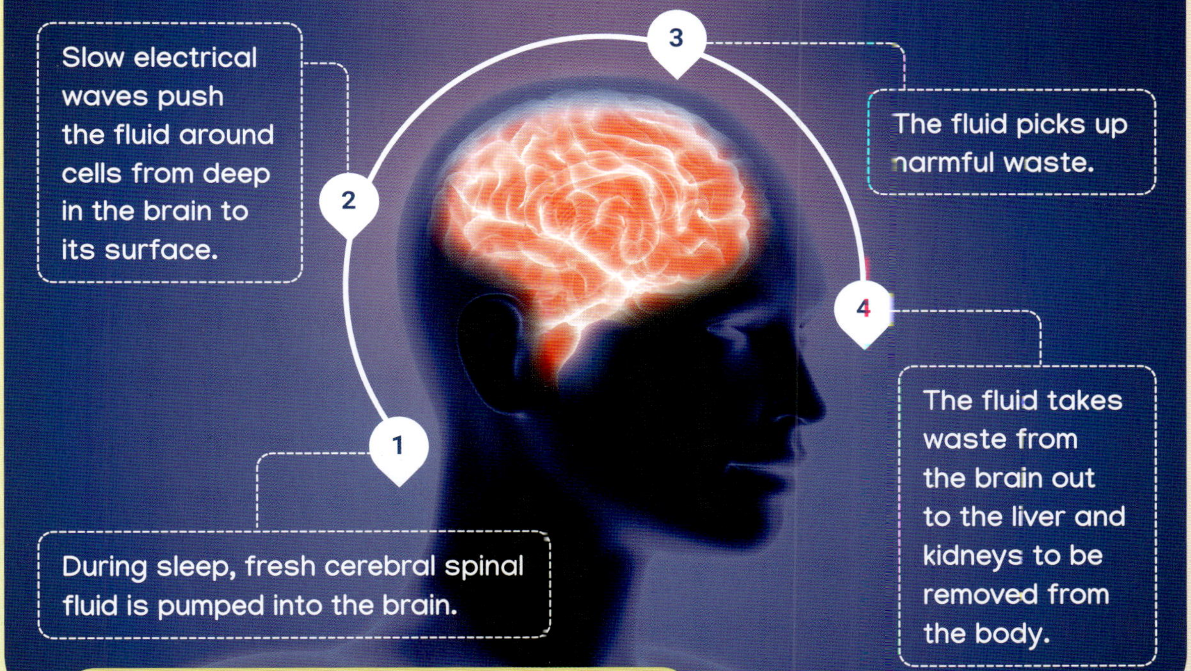

1. During sleep, fresh cerebral spinal fluid is pumped into the brain.
2. Slow electrical waves push the fluid around cells from deep in the brain to its surface.
3. The fluid picks up harmful waste.
4. The fluid takes waste from the brain out to the liver and kidneys to be removed from the body.

Fluid from the spine is sent into the brain to clean it through the glymphatic system.

SLEEP FACT

Scientists think there are things we can all do to make our glymphatic systems work more effectively. These include exercising regularly; eating foods rich in **magnesium** such as nuts, fruits and vegetables; and reducing day-to-day stress in our lives.

Technology and Sleep

Today, technology can help us improve our sleep. It can also help us work out what's going wrong if we have problems with our sleep.

Tracking Our Sleep at Home

Using digital devices, we can **monitor** and improve our sleep at home. For example, apps on our phones or other devices can track how well we are sleeping.

Some apps monitor sleep through a wearable item, such as a finger ring or a smartwatch, that records the wearer's heart rate, breathing, movements and body temperature. Other apps can work on devices like smartphones that are left beside the bed during sleep, using sonar and the phone's microphone. All of these apps can help us learn more about our own sleep patterns and find ways to improve our sleep.

Sleeping with electronic devices nearby or wearing watches while sleeping may not be suitable for everyone.

Smartwatches can measure our heart rate while we sleep.

Other apps improve sleep by helping us relax at bedtime. These apps might play relaxing music or meditations that can put us in a calm state of mind. For example, they might help us imagine that we're in a relaxing place, like a garden, or walking by the sea.

There are even apps that play "white noise" to help people get to sleep. White noise is a sound like a continuous "shhhh" that can hide other distracting noises and soothe the listener. It is often used to soothe crying babies and help them go to sleep. These apps can play other types of soothing sounds, too, like the sound of rain, ocean waves or the hum of a fan.

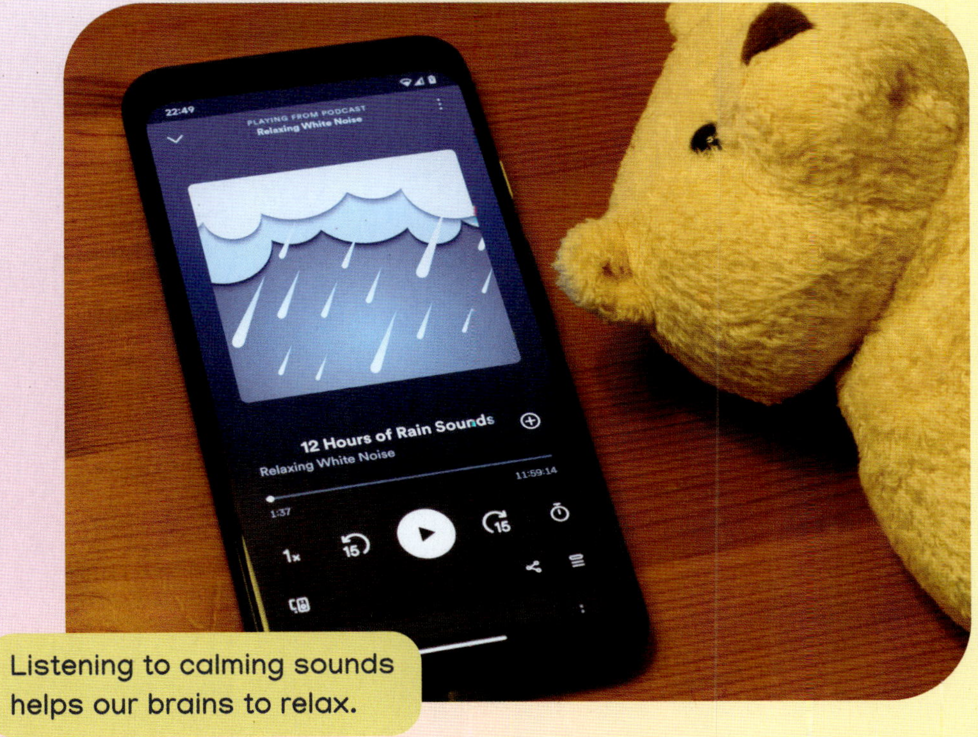

Listening to calming sounds helps our brains to relax.

SLEEP FACT

Some people think that babies like white noise because it's similar to the sounds they would have heard before they were born. It's very noisy inside a human body, and babies can find the noise familiar and relaxing.

Sleep Clinics

When people are having trouble getting to sleep, or are not sleeping well, their doctor might send them to a sleep clinic to find out what's causing the problem. A sleep clinic uses technology to investigate conditions such as snoring, and difficulties in staying asleep.

Scientists at sleep clinics can measure how effectively we sleep and check for problems.

One common condition sleep clinics investigate is called sleep apnoea (pronounced *ap-nee-ah*). When a person suffers from sleep apnoea, their airways collapse as they sleep. This causes their breathing to keep stopping and starting during the night. They might stop breathing for ten seconds or longer and snore loudly. They may also wake several times during the night. This condition can affect the person's sleep so much that they might need to sleep during the day. It can also contribute to other health problems, such as heart problems, **diabetes** and high **blood pressure**.

When airways close because of sleep apnoea, the body and the brain don't get the air they need.

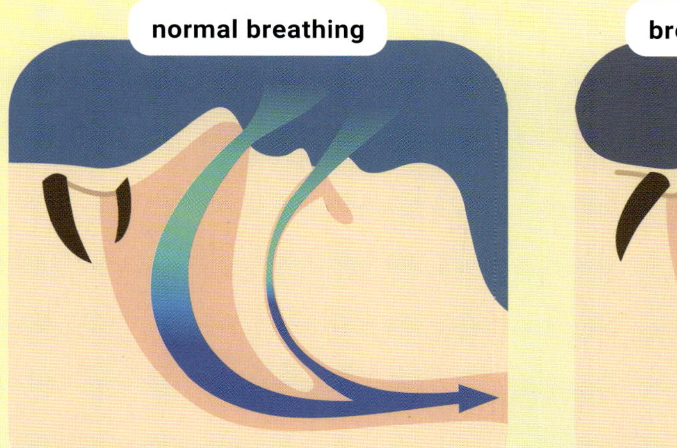

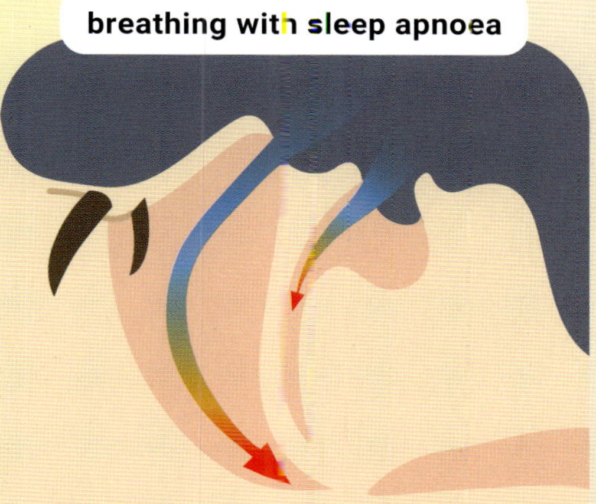

When someone has sleep apnoea, their muscles relax too much and block their airway.

SLEEP FACT

It's quite normal for us to wake at least two or three times during the night between sleep cycles. Often, we might not even remember waking up.

In a sleep clinic, patients are monitored closely as they sleep so that doctors can see if anything unusual is happening. Patients usually spend a night at the clinic. The staff at the clinic attach **sensors** to various parts of the patient's body, including the chest, head, face, legs and fingers. The sensors measure a range of body functions as the patient sleeps. These include heart rate and **rhythm**, brain activity, movements and breathing.

A sleep doctor reads an EEG graph to check how well a patient is sleeping.

Sensors measure a man's breathing and brain activity at a sleep clinic.

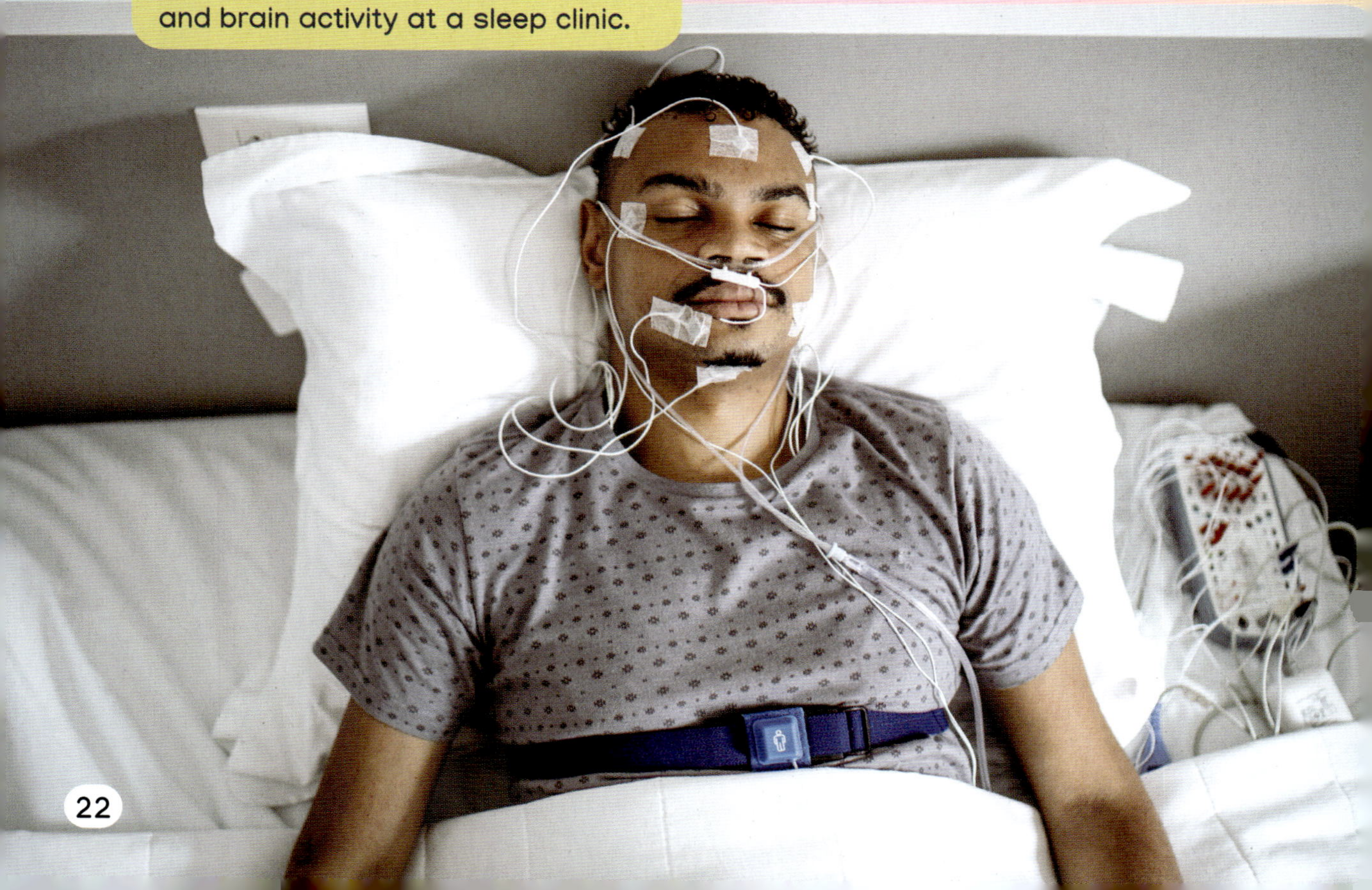

The information collected by the sensors can help the patient's doctor work out what is causing their sleep problems. It can also tell the doctor about the patient's quality of sleep: for example, how many times the patient wakes during the night. If the doctor thinks their patient is suffering from sleep apnoea, technology can help them, too. Special machines can be fitted to the patient's face overnight and send air into their nose and mouth to keep their airways open as they sleep.

Sleep apnoea machines prevent airways from closing by making sure there is a steady flow of air into our lungs while we sleep.

Lots Left to Learn

Although scientists have studied sleep for a long time, there is still a lot left to discover about it. These are a few of the big questions scientists are trying to answer about sleep.

Why Do We Dream?

Many scientists believe dreaming may strengthen our memories, so that we can remember things better when we are awake. Dreaming might also allow us to experience different emotions and situations in our heads, so that we are better prepared to deal with them if they happen in real life. Some scientists also think it's possible that dreaming might just be something that happens during sleep, and that it may not serve any particular purpose.

What Is the Purpose of Rapid Eye Movement (REM) Sleep?

The full purpose of REM sleep is still unknown. It's believed to play a role in helping us to process our emotions, but scientists think it may also be important for the development of our brains. They believe this because babies spend a lot of time in REM sleep, and it's during REM sleep that many important connections are made between the cells in our brains.

Unlike older children and adults, babies move around during REM sleep.

Why Do Some People Need More or Less Sleep than Others?

Some people seem to need a lot more, or a lot less, sleep than other people. They might sleep for two or three hours longer, or shorter, than most people. This doesn't seem to affect their health or cause any other problems, but scientists aren't sure what causes these differences between people.

People's brains often sleep best at different times of the day as well, with some people needing to sleep earlier at night or later into the morning than others.

Some people can still think clearly with just a few hours of sleep each night. One such person was the inventor Thomas Edison, who claimed he only slept for three or four hours each night. Edison was able to invent important things like the light bulb and the first sound recording machine.

How to Sleep Well

There are a number of things we can do to give ourselves the best chance of having a good sleep and get all of the benefits sleep can give us.

1 Set a regular sleep schedule. In other words, try to go to bed at the same time each night, and wake up at a similar time each morning – including on weekends. This helps your body to develop a sleep pattern, which makes going to sleep easier, and gives you a better quality of sleep, too.

Alarm clocks are a great tool to help you wake up at the same time every day.

2 Avoid **vigorous** exercise in the last few hours before bedtime. Getting plenty of exercise during the day helps us to sleep better, but exercising too close to our bedtime can make our body temperature too high. This makes it harder to get to sleep, and to sleep well.

Your body needs time to wind down after playing sport.

3 Avoid foods or drinks that contain **caffeine** for at least four hours before bedtime. Caffeine makes the brain more active. It's found in chocolate and drinks such as tea, coffee, energy drinks and some soft drinks.

Food and drinks with caffeine stop your brain from telling you that you feel sleepy.

4. Enjoy some relaxing activities before bedtime, such as taking a warm bath, reading or listening to calming music. This will help you to wind down, and helps your brain to produce a hormone called **melatonin** which makes you sleepy.

Reading a book is a great way to relax your brain.

5. Avoid bright lights and loud sounds that keep your brain alert for one to two hours before bedtime. These can come from loud music, gaming consoles or TVs, and it can help to not have these in your bedroom.

Watching videos or playing games makes your brain alert instead of relaxed.

6. Avoid playing on screen devices such as phones and tablets for one to two hours before bedtime, too. The type of light screens use, known as **blue light**, can wake your brain up, instead of helping it go to sleep.

7 Make sure your bedroom is a comfortable temperature, and that it's dark when the lights are off. Darkness also helps your brain to produce melatonin to make you sleepy. Your room doesn't need to be pitch dark. Many people find that a soft night light can help them to sleep as well.

Night lights come in all different shapes, so you can pick something that makes you feel happy and calm.

8 If you're finding it difficult to get to sleep, it's often better to get out of bed and read a book or do another gentle activity, like stretches, until you feel yourself becoming sleepy.

SLEEP FACT

Good sleep is important for animals, too, although they often sleep very differently from humans! The sperm whale, for example, sleeps in an upright position in the water, in a group of other sperm whales.

Time Well Spent

Sleep is vital to our health and happiness, as well as our development as we grow. Without a good night's sleep, it's difficult to concentrate on study or work, or to fully enjoy the activities we do for fun. It's worth making an effort to sleep well each night. Good sleep is time very well spent!

Try to get a good night's sleep so you can wake up each morning feeling happy and well-rested.

Glossary

Alzheimer's disease (*noun*)	a disease in the brain that causes loss of memory and a loss of the ability to perform simple tasks
bacteria (*noun*)	tiny living things that sometimes cause disease
blood pressure (*noun*)	a measurement of how hard the heart is working to push blood around the body
blue light (*noun*)	a kind of bright light that comes from the Sun and digital screens
caffeine (*noun*)	a chemical found in food and drinks that makes you feel more awake
cells (*noun*)	the smallest parts that make up all living things
consume (*verb*)	to eat or drink something
diabetes (*noun*)	a disease where the body is unable to control the amount of sugar in a person's blood
essential (*noun*)	very important
glymphatic system (*noun*)	a waste removal system in the brain and spine
hormones (*noun*)	chemicals that help bodies grow and that send messages through the body
immune system (*noun*)	a natural system inside the body that protects against diseases and poisons
magnesium (*noun*)	a mineral used by the body to help maintain muscles, nerves and bones
melatonin (*noun*)	a natural substance produced by the human body that makes us feel tired
monitor (*verb*)	to watch carefully over a period of time
mood (*noun*)	the way a person is feeling at a particular time
overwhelmed (*adjective*)	feeling an emotion that is too strong to deal with
Parkinson's disease (*noun*)	a disease in the brain and nervous system that weakens muscles
perception (*noun*)	a person's ability to use their sense of sight, hearing, taste, touch and smell
processes (*noun*)	a series of steps needed to create a specific result
quality (*adjective*)	used to describe the standard of something
rhythm (*noun*)	a repeating pattern of sound or movement

temporarily (*adverb*)	for a short time; not permanently
sensors (*noun*)	devices that detect and measure where and how much of something there is, such as a person's heartbeat
vigorous (*adjective*)	energetic or forceful
viruses (*noun*)	tiny living things that can only grow by living in something else
vivid (*adjective*)	something very bright or clear

Index